The Atlas of the Seven Continents™

NORTH AMERICA

Wendy Vierow

The Rosen Publishing Group's
PowerKids Press™
New York

For Chris, who loves atlases

Published in 2004 by The Rosen Publishing Group, Inc.
29 East 21st Street, New York, NY 10010

Copyright © 2004 by The Rosen Publishing Group, Inc.

First Edition

Editor: Frances E. Ruffin
Book Design: Maria E. Melendez
Book Layout: Eric DePalo

Photo Credits: Cover and title page, map of North America, pp. 5, 11 (bottom left), 12 (top right) © Earth Observatory/NASA; p. 7 © 2001 Todd Marshall; p. 14 (top right) © 1997 Cartesia; pp. 9 (map symbols), 15 (map of North America) illustrated by Eric DePalo; pp. 9, 11, 13, 17 (map of North America), 19 (left maps), 21 (left maps) © GeoAtlas; p. 17 (squirrel monkey) © Steve Kaufman/CORBIS; p. 19 (New Anchors) © Roger Ressmeyer/CORBIS; p. 19 (rancher with horses) © Martin Rogers/CORBIS; p. 19 (men on floating logs) © Annie Griffiths Belt; p. 21 (little boys) © Royalty-Free/CORBIS; p. 21 (Eskimo woman) © Galen Rowell/CORBIS; p. 21 (boys on bicycles) © Bob Krist/CORBIS.

Vierow, Wendy.
North America / Wendy Vierow.
   v. cm. — (The atlas of the seven continents)
Includes bibliographical references and index.
Contents: Earth's continents and oceans — North America long ago — How to read a map — Natural wonders of North America — Countries of North America — The climate of North America — Plants and animals of North America — Making a living in North America — The people of North America — A scientist in North America.
ISBN 13: 978-1-4358-3699-0
1. North America—Geography—Juvenile literature. 2. North America—Maps for children. [1. North America—Maps.] I. Title.
E40.5 .V54 2004
917—dc21

                         2002154685

Manufactured in the United States of America

Contents

Earth's Continents and Oceans

North America is the third-largest continent, after Asia and Africa. A continent is a large body of land. The seven continents on Earth are Africa, Antarctica, Asia, Australia, Europe, North America, and South America. Scientists think that, more than 200 million years ago, the continents were part of one giant continent called Pangaea. They believe that movement by Earth's **plates** caused Pangaea to break into smaller continents. Today Earth's moving plates cause **earthquakes**, such as those along California's San Andreas Fault. A fault is a place where two plates push together. Moving plates also pull apart to let melted rock rise and form new land, as shown by the volcanoes of the Hawaiian Islands. Scientists also believe that long ago there was one ocean called Panthalassa. Today there are four oceans on Earth. To the west of North America lies the world's largest ocean, the Pacific. To the east of North America is the world's second-largest ocean, the Atlantic. The Arctic Ocean, Earth's smallest ocean, borders North America to the north. The Indian Ocean does not touch the continent of North America.

Arctic Ocean

Asia

Europe

North America

Atlantic Ocean

Africa

South America

Indian Ocean

Australia

Pacific Ocean

Antarctica

PERMIAN
286-245 million years ago

PANGAEA

Equator

TRIASSIC
245-208 million years ago

Equator

JURASSIC
208-144 million years ago

Equator

CRETACEOUS
144-66 million years ago

Equator

PRESENT DAY
From 66 million years ago

NORTH AMERICA

EUROPE ASIA

AFRICA

SOUTH AMERICA

Equator

AUSTRALIA

ANTARCTICA

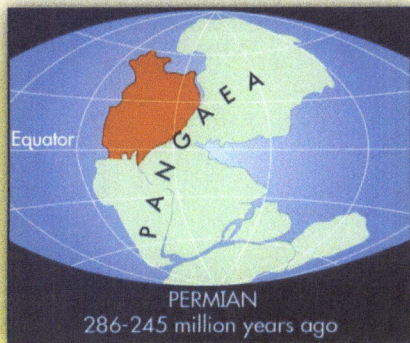

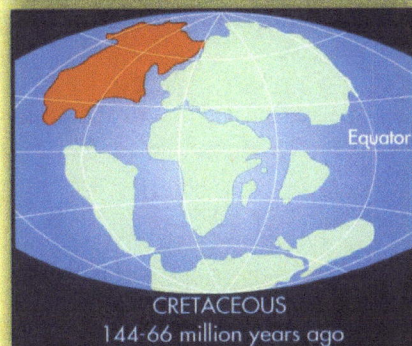

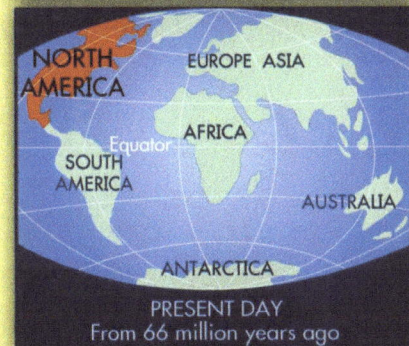

Top: *This photograph of the continents was taken from space. The five small maps, above and right, show how North America, in red, might have been formed when the huge continent of Pangaea broke apart.*

Dinosaurs and huge reptiles lived in North America during the Mesozoic **era**, or the Age of Dinosaurs, which lasted from about 240 million to 66 million years ago. In the Mesozoic era, elasmosaurs swam in North America's waters hunting for fish. These long-necked reptiles were 36-feet (11-m) long. In the air diving for fish was the pteranodon, a large flying reptile that measured 23 feet (7 m) from wing tip to wing tip. On the ground searching for meat was a 20-inch-long (50-cm-long) **marsupial** called a *Didelphodon*.

Dinosaurs included the 40-foot-long (12-m-long) meat-eating *Tyrannosaurus rex*, which may have run up to 25 miles per hour (40 km/h). The seismosaur was a dinosaur that measured up to 115 feet (35 m) high. With its long neck, it could eat the leaves of tall trees. Stegosaurs, dinosaurs that were 30 feet (9 m) long with two rows of pointed spikes on their backs, also ate plants. Plants of the Mesozoic era included ginkgoes, conifer trees, which are trees with cones, and cycads, or trees that looked like palms or ferns. The first flowering plants also appeared during the Mesozoic era.

A Tyrannosaurus rex *chases a pair of Chirostenotes. Tyrannosaurus rex, often called the tyrant lizard king, walked on two powerful legs and had a huge head with large teeth. Chirostenotes were smaller, but were about the same size as adult humans. They moved quickly to catch smaller animals for food. Fossils, or hardened remains, of both have been found in western North America.*

How to Read a Map

You can find different kinds of maps in an atlas. Maps have special features that make them easy to read. To find out the subject of a map, look at its title. The title is often found in a box called the map key or the legend. This box tells what the **symbols** on the map mean. The map may also have a map scale, which shows how distances on a map compare to real distances on Earth.

Most maps have a compass rose or a north pointer that shows direction on the map. The four main directions on Earth are north, south, east, and west. North is the direction toward the North Pole. **Longitude** lines and **latitude** lines also show direction. All longitude lines meet at the North Pole and the South Pole. The **prime meridian** is 0° longitude. The **equator**, which is 0° latitude, is the boundary line between the Northern **Hemisphere** and the Southern Hemisphere. North America is entirely in the Northern Hemisphere. In the Northern Hemisphere, the seasons differ from those in the Southern Hemisphere by about six months. When it is winter in Montreal, Canada, it is summer in Buenos Aires, Argentina.

NORTH AMERICA: LANDMARKS

180°w 165°w 150°w 135°w 120°w 105°w 90°w 75°w 60°w 45°w 30°w

ARCTIC OCEAN

75°n

Baffin Bay

Beaufort Sea

60°n

Bering Sea

Gulf of Alaska

Hudson Bay

45°n

PACIFIC OCEAN

ATLANTIC OCEAN

Longitude Lines

N

30°n

Latitude Lines

15°n

Gulf of Mexico

Caribbean Sea

NORTH AMERICA
MERCATOR PROJECTION
0 km   500   1000   1500 km
scale at the Equator
GEOATLAS® - © 2001 Graphi-Ogre

180°w 165°w 150°w 135°w 120°w 105°w 90°w 75°w 60°w 45°w 30°w

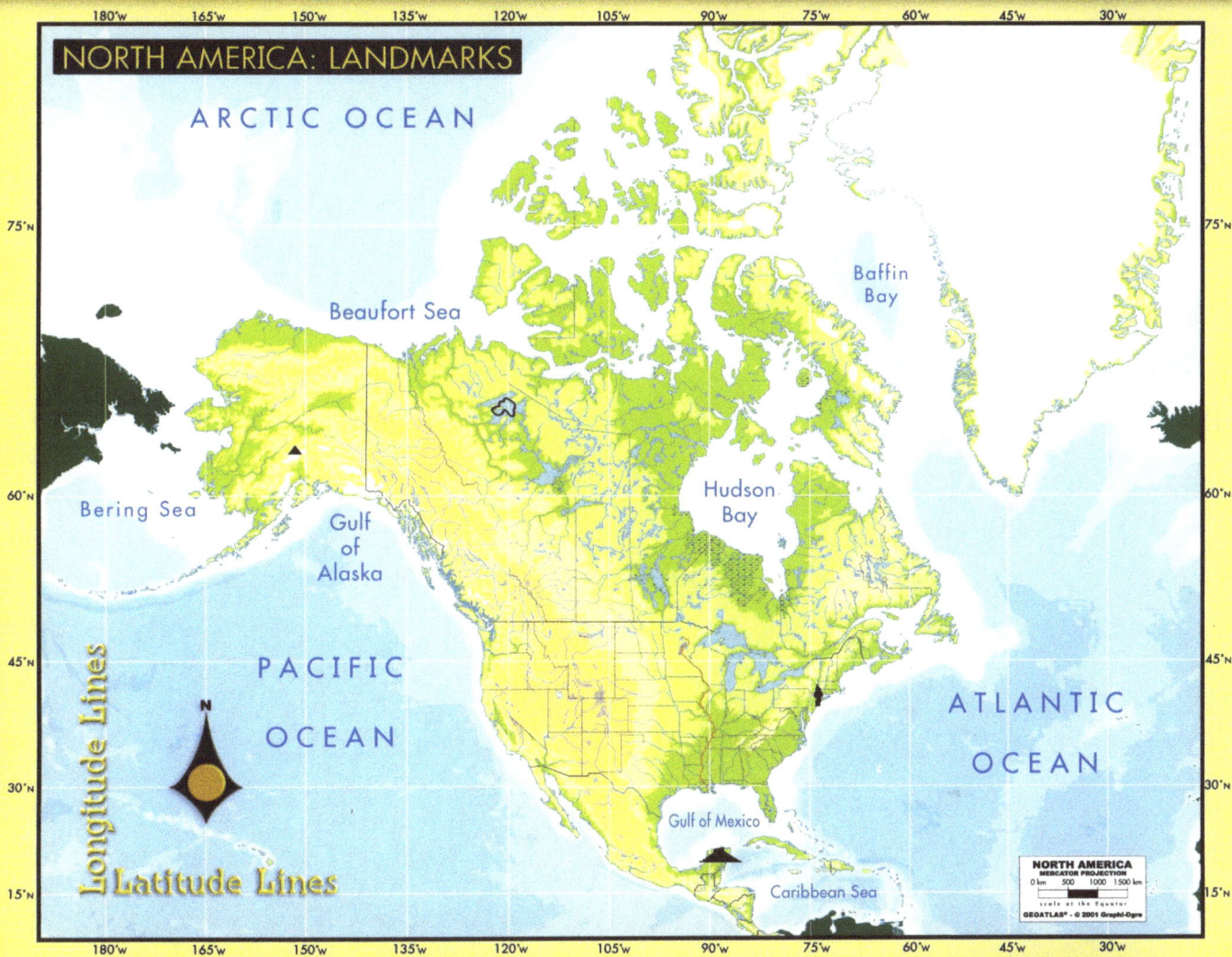

MAP KEY NORTH AMERICA: LANDMARKS

| Statue of Liberty | Mississippi River | Mount McKinley | Great Bear Lake | Chichén Itzá |

Natural Wonders of North America

North America's coastline, which includes many islands, is the longest of any continent's at about 190,000 miles (305,775 km). The islands of North America range from Earth's largest island, Greenland, in the north to the sunny southern Caribbean islands in the south. The Rocky Mountains form North America's longest mountain chain. They run for 3,000 miles (4,828 km) from Alaska to New Mexico. The continent's highest mountain is Mount McKinley in the Alaska Range at 20,320 feet (6,194 m). The lowest point is California's Death Valley, at 282 feet (86 m) below **sea level**. The Grand Canyon, at about 1 mile (2 km) deep and 280 miles (451 km) long, is the world's largest canyon. North America contains the world's largest freshwater lake, Lake Superior, which borders Canada and the United States and covers 31,800 square miles (82,362 sq km). In the United States, the system of the Mississippi, Missouri, and Ohio Rivers is North America's longest at about 4,700 miles (7,564 km).

NORTH AMERICA: LAND and WATER

ARCTIC OCEAN

Ellesmere Island

Queen
Elizabeth
Islands

GREENLAND
(Denmark)

Chukchi
Sea

Beaufort
Sea

Banks
Island

Baffin
Bay

Brooks Range

Victoria
Island

Baffin Island

Bering Strait

Yukon

Yukon

Mackenzie

Great
Bear Lake

Yukon

Kuzo

Mt McKinley

Great Slave
Lake

Hudson
Bay

Labrador
Sea

Bering Sea

Coast Mountains

Rocky Mountains

N. Saskatchewan

Lake
Winnipeg

St Lawrence

Island of
Newfoundland

Kodiak
Island

Gulf
of
Alaska

Queen
Charlotte
Islands

S.Saskatchewan

Nova
Scotia

Aleutian Islands

Vancouver
Island

Columbia

Columbia

Missouri

Lake Superior

Lake
Michigan

Lake Ontario

Cascade Range

Snake

Great Salt
Lake

Great Plains

Lake
Huron

Lake Erie

Mojave Desert

Colorado

Ohio

Appalachian Mts

Death Valley

Grand Canyon

Arkansas

Coastal Plain

Sonoran Desert

Mississippi

Baja California

Rio Grande

BERMUDA

ATLANTIC

Sierra
Madre
Oriental

Gulf of
Mexico

Lake Okeechobee

THE BAHAMAS

OCEAN

Yucatán

CUBA

DOMINICAN REPUBLIC

PACIFIC

JAMAICA

HAITI

PUERTO RICO

OCEAN

Caribbean Sea

Mosquito Coast
Panama
Canal

N

180°w 165°w 150°w 135°w 120°w 105°w 90°w 75°w 60°w 45°w 30°w

75°N

60°N

45°N

30°N

15°N

Countries of North America

This photograph of Central America was taken from high above Earth.

Most of North America is made up of the countries of Canada and the United States of America. Canada is the world's second-largest country in area, after Russia. The United States, which is made up of 50 states, is the world's fourth-largest country in area. The United States has a population of 286,067,000. Greenland, surrounded by the Atlantic and Arctic Oceans, is only 10 miles (16 km) from Canada. Greenland is part of North America, but it is also a **province** of Denmark, a country in Europe. South of Canada and the United States is the country of Mexico. Mexico City, the capital of Mexico, is one of the world's most-populated cities with more than 18 million people. South of Mexico is an area of North America known as Central America. Central American countries include Belize, Costa Rica, El Salvador, Guatemala, Honduras, Nicaragua, and Panama. Also part of North America are the sunny, warm West Indies islands that stretch about 2,000 miles (3,219 km), north to south, in the Caribbean Sea.

NORTH AMERICA: COUNTRIES and CAPITAL CITIES

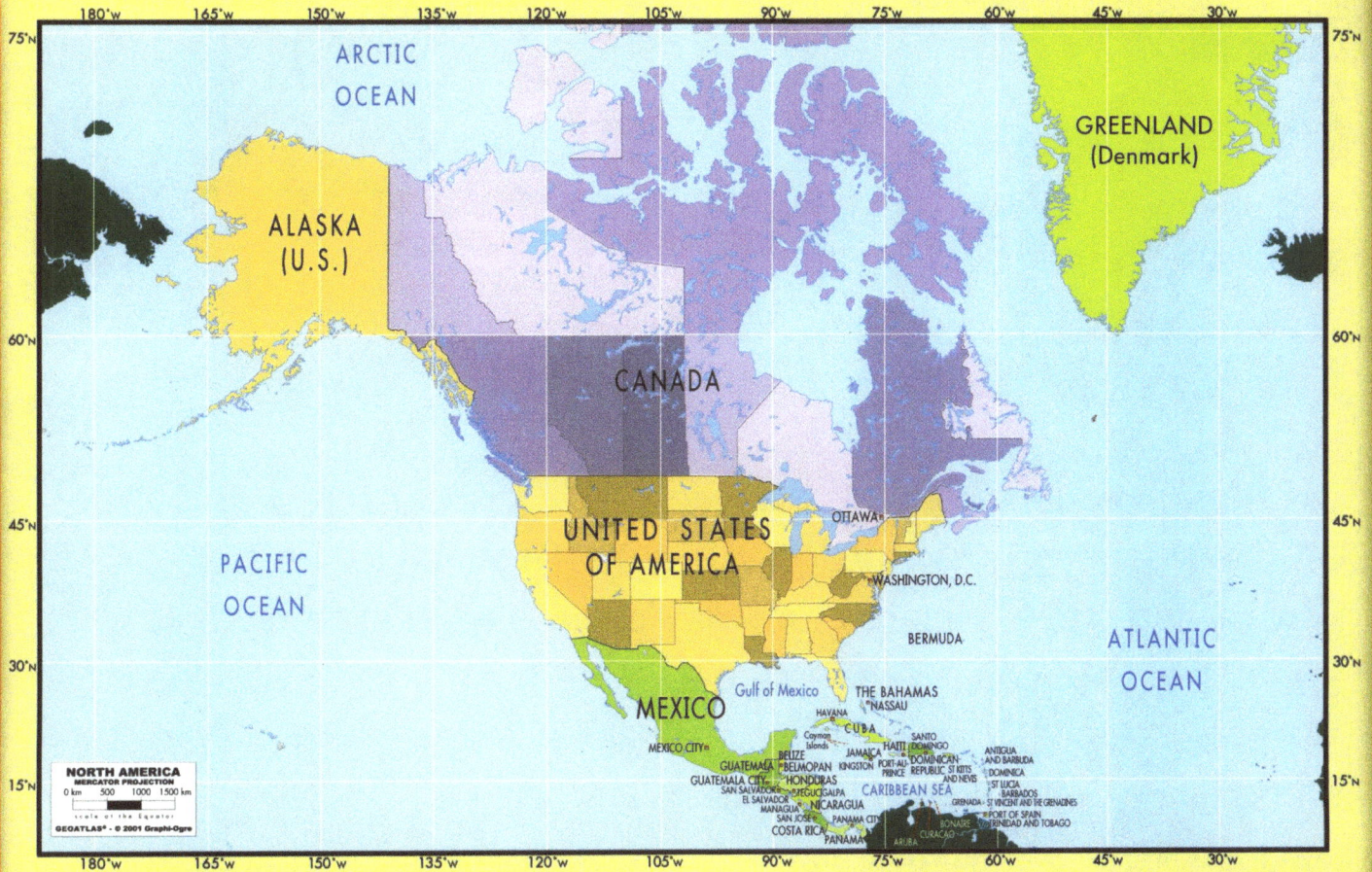

ARCTIC OCEAN

GREENLAND (Denmark)

ALASKA (U.S.)

CANADA

PACIFIC OCEAN

UNITED STATES OF AMERICA

OTTAWA

WASHINGTON, D.C.

BERMUDA

ATLANTIC OCEAN

Gulf of Mexico

THE BAHAMAS
NASSAU

MEXICO

HAVANA

CUBA

Cayman Islands

SANTO DOMINGO

ANTIGUA AND BARBUDA

MEXICO CITY

GUATEMALA

BELIZE
BELMOPAN

JAMAICA

HAITI

KINGSTON

PORT-AU-PRINCE

DOMINICAN REPUBLIC

ST KITTS AND NEVIS

DOMINICA

GUATEMALA CITY

HONDURAS

ST LUCIA

SAN SALVADOR

TEGUCIGALPA

BARBADOS

EL SALVADOR

MANAGUA

NICARAGUA

GRENADA

ST VINCENT AND THE GRENADINES

CARIBBEAN SEA

SAN JOSE

PANAMA CITY

PORT OF SPAIN

TRINIDAD AND TOBAGO

COSTA RICA

PANAMA

BONAIRE

ARUBA

CURACAO

NORTH AMERICA
MERCATOR PROJECTION
0 km   500   1000 1500 km
scale at the Equator
GEOATLAS® - © 2001 Graphi-Ogre

North America's Largest Capital Cities

■ Capital Cities

Havana, Cuba
2,180,000

Mexico City, Mexico
18,000,000

Toronto, Canada
4,264,000

Santo Domingo, Dominican Republic
2,150,000

Guatemala, Guatemala
1,700,000

Managua, Nicaragua
974,000

Port-au-Prince, Haiti
700,000

Washington, D.C., United States
572,000

Europe-Owned Islands

Greenland
(Denmark)

Aruba
(Netherlands)

Cayman Islands
(United Kingdom)

Curacao
(Netherlands)

Bonaire
(Netherlands)

The Climate of North America

North America is the only continent that has every kind of climate on Earth, from Greenland's freezing **ice cap** climate to the warm **tropical** climate of the West Indies. Climate includes temperature, or how hot or cold a place is, and precipitation, or how much moisture falls from the sky. Northern Canada has cold winters and cool summers. However, most of North America has cold winters and warm summers with **moderate** precipitation. In the southern part of North America, the winters are warmer and the summers are hotter. This is because latitude affects climate. Places on Earth closest to the equator are warm and wet. In Central America there are **rain forests** with warm, wet climates near the equator. Elevation, or how high a place is, also affects climate. Most places at high elevations have a cool, wet climate. For example, in Panama, temperatures average about 66°F (19°C) in the mountains, but they average about 80°F (27°C) in lower land.

The continent of North America has many climates.

14

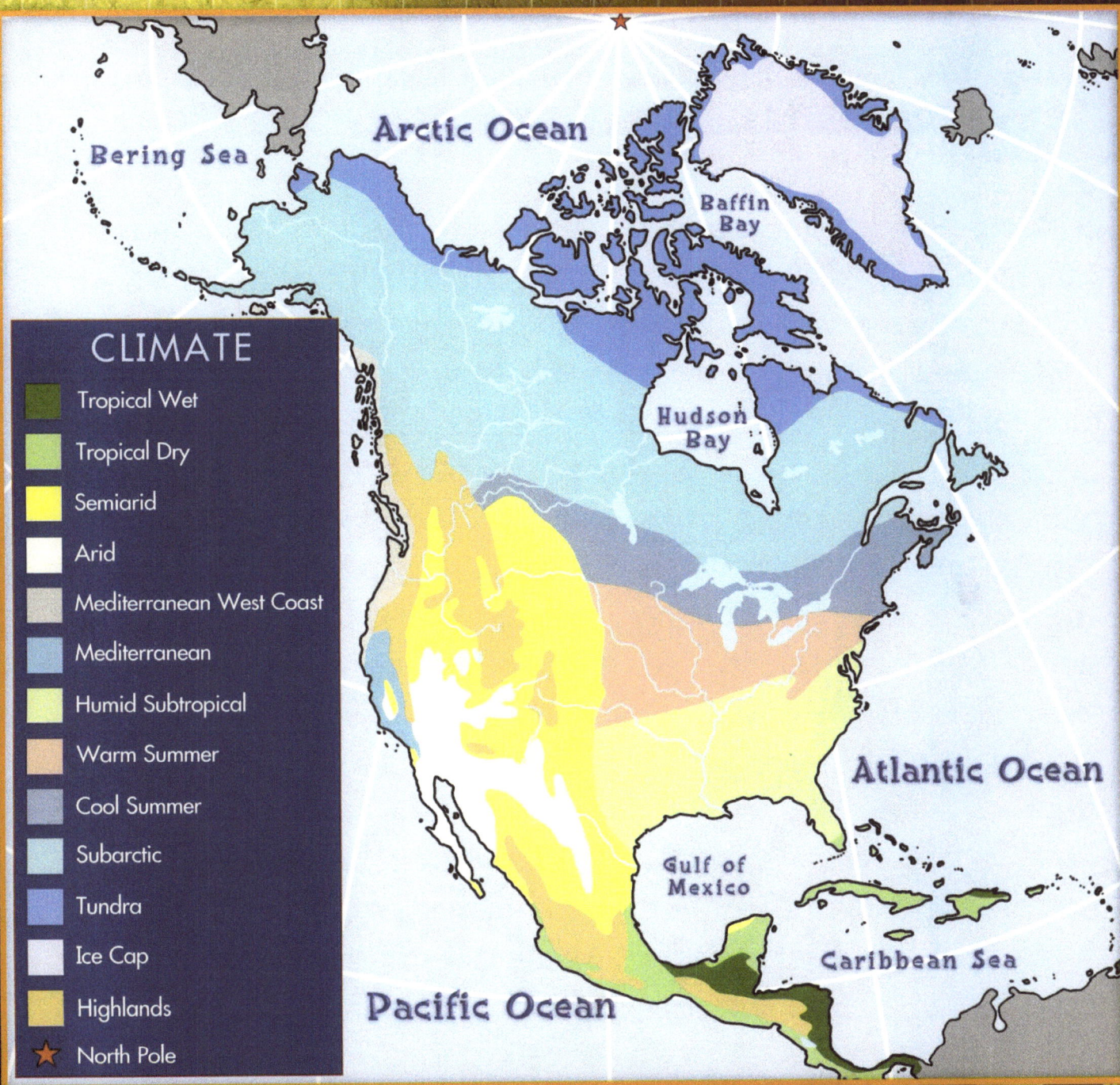

CLIMATE

- ⬛ (dark green) Tropical Wet
- ⬛ (light green) Tropical Dry
- ⬛ (yellow) Semiarid
- ⬛ (white) Arid
- ⬛ (gray) Mediterranean West Coast
- ⬛ (blue-gray) Mediterranean
- ⬛ (pale green) Humid Subtropical
- ⬛ (tan/pink) Warm Summer
- ⬛ (gray-blue) Cool Summer
- ⬛ (pale cyan) Subarctic
- ⬛ (blue) Tundra
- ⬛ (pale lavender) Ice Cap
- ⬛ (tan) Highlands
- ★ North Pole

Bering Sea

Arctic Ocean

Baffin Bay

Hudson Bay

Atlantic Ocean

Gulf of Mexico

Caribbean Sea

Pacific Ocean

North America's Plants and Animals

North America has many different kinds of plants and animals. A variety of bears, such as polar, black, and brown bears, including grizzly bears, make their homes in North America. The world's largest meat-eating land animal is the Alaskan brown bear. It is about 9 feet (2.7 m) tall and weighs up to 1,700 pounds (771 kg). Seals and whales swim in northern waters. Near the Arctic Ocean, grasses and mosses grow. Fir, pine, and spruce trees fill the Canadian forests. Giant redwood trees grow along the Pacific coast. The world's tallest-known living tree is a redwood in California that stands 368 feet (112 m) high. A bristlecone pine tree in California is the world's oldest-known living tree at 4,600 years old. Also in California is the largest flying bird in North America, the California condor. This bird is from 8 to 9 ½ feet (2–3 m) long from wing tip to wing tip and weighs up to 23 pounds (10 kg). White-tailed deer can be found in most parts of North America, except in the deserts. Rain forests in Central America, where jaguars and monkeys live, have among the greatest variety of plants and animals on Earth.

An Alaskan brown bear snaps up a salmon.

This mother squirrel monkey carries her baby on her back.

This parrot lives in a Central American rain forest.

Fifty million bison once lived in North America. Today 200,000 roam America's Great Plains.

California's redwood trees are the tallest trees in the world.

Red foxes hunt in many places in North America, from forests to cities.

Making a Living in North America

Although only 4 percent of the workers in the United States and Canada are farmers, they grow enough food to feed their countries, with extra to sell to other countries. In Mexico and Central America, about 50 percent of all workers farm. Most Central American farmers do not own their own land. Many work on plantations, or large farms, raising crops that include bananas, coffee, and cotton.

After Europe, North America produces more manufactured goods than any other continent, including automobiles, **chemical products**, and food products. About one of every five workers in North America has a job in manufacturing. Most people in the United States and Canada work in service jobs in fields such as finance, education, **real estate**, and **communications**. Canada leads the world in **timber** production. Lumber, paper, and other products are made from Canada's trees. Although less than 1 percent of North American workers are in the mining business, North America has many important **natural resources**, including coal, oil, and natural gas.

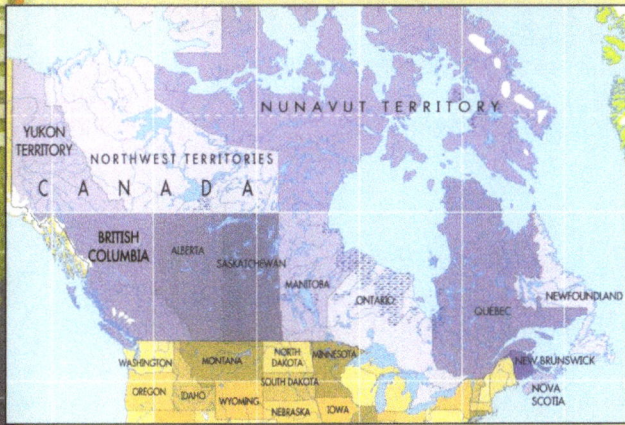

Workers in Canada's British Columbia load logs onto a ship.

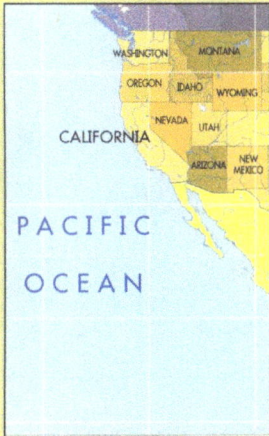

These newspeople in San Francisco, California, are reporting the news on television.

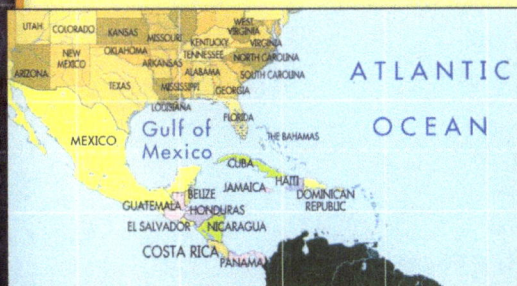

A farmer leads his horses on a ranch in Costa Rica.

The People of North America

Scientists think that people first came to North America from Asia between 15,000 and 35,000 years ago. They were the **ancestors** of today's Native Americans. In Mexico, Native Americans, including the **Aztecs**, built great civilizations, or communities. These civilizations lasted until the arrival of Europeans in the 1500s. European settlers forced Native Americans and people from Africa to work as slaves in North America until slavery was made illegal in the late 1800s. During the early 1800s, many people from Europe began to move to North America for a better life. Most came to live in the United States, but others moved to Canada. In the mid-1800s, news of gold in California brought Chinese **immigrants** to the United States. In the 1900s, jobs in factories and on farms brought people from eastern and southern Europe to the United States and Canada. Today, most people who move to the United States come from places that include the North American countries of Cuba, the Dominican Republic, Jamaica, and Mexico. Also, many are coming from countries in Asia and the eastern European country of Ukraine.

ALASKA (U.S.)

YUKON TERRITORY

NORTHWEST TERRITORIES

C A N A D A

BRITISH COLUMBIA   ALBERTA

SASKATCHEWAN

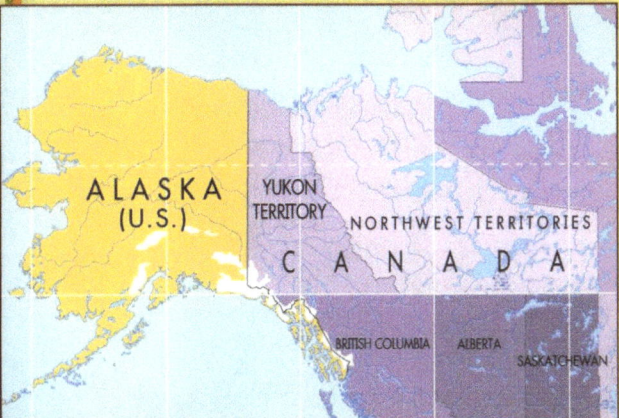

This Native American woman is dressed in a fur parka, or jacket, to keep warm in the freezing climate of Barrow, Alaska.

UNITED STATES OF AMERICA

ATLANTIC OCEAN

PACIFIC OCEAN

MEXICO   Gulf of Mexico

THE BAHAMAS

CUBA

JAMAICA   HAITI   DOMINICAN REPUBLIC

BELIZE

GUATEMALA   HONDURAS

EL SALVADOR   NICARAGUA

COSTA RICA

PANAMA

These boys, who live in the U.S. state of New Jersey, are going to fish.

ATLANTIC OCEAN

MEXICO   Gulf of Mexico

THE BAHAMAS

CUBA

PACIFIC OCEAN

JAMAICA   HAITI

BELIZE   DOMINICAN REPUBLIC

GUATEMALA   HONDURAS

EL SALVADOR   NICARAGUA

COSTA RICA

PANAMA

These young Mexican boys share a laugh in a doorway.

A Scientist in North America

Lucy Jones is a seismologist, or a scientist who studies earthquakes. She is scientist-in-charge of the United States Geological Survey (USGS) in southern California. One thing that Jones studies is aftershocks, or smaller earthquakes that happen after a larger earthquake hits an area. Jones helps to estimate, or guess, where aftershocks will occur and what harm they might cause. This helps emergency workers, such as the police and fire departments, know where to send help. In 2002, Governor Gray Davis of California made Jones part of a special commission, or group, on earthquake safety. The commission helps to find ways to make living with earthquakes safer. Jones is in charge of the USGS office in Pasadena, California. This office has special instruments that tell about earthquake movement. These instruments can tell when an earthquake is happening, and how strong the movements of the earthquake are. Lucy Jones wrote a book called *Earthquake ABC* for children and their parents.

Glossary

ancestors (AN-ses-terz) Relatives who lived long ago.

Aztecs (AZ-teks) Native Americans of central Mexico.

chemical (KEH-mih-kul) Relating to matter that can be mixed with other matter to cause changes.

communications (kuh-myoo-nih-KAY-shunz) The sharing of facts or feelings.

earthquakes (URTH-kwayks) Shakings of Earth's crust because of the movement of large pieces of land, called plates, that run into each other.

equator (ih-KWAY-tur) An imaginary circle around the middle of Earth.

era (ER-uh) A period of time or history.

hemisphere (HEH-muh-sfeer) One half of Earth or another sphere.

ice cap (EYES KAP) A huge layer of ice and snow that covers a large area of land.

immigrants (IH-muh-grints) People who move to a new country from another country.

latitude (LA-tih-tood) The distance north or south of the equator, measured by degrees.

longitude (LON-jih-tood) The distance east or west of the prime meridian, measured by degrees.

marsupial (mar-SOO-pee-ul) A type of animal that carries its young in a pouch.

moderate (MAH-duh-ret) Tending toward the average.

natural resources (NA-chuh-rul REE-sors-ez) Things in nature, such as water, rock, and trees, that can be used by people.

plates (PLAYTS) The moving pieces of Earth's crust, the top layer of Earth.

prime meridian (PRYM meh-RIH–dee-en) The imaginary line that passes through Greenwich, England, and that is 0° longitude.

products (PRAH-dukts) Things produced.

province (PRAH-vins) One of the main parts of a country.

rain forests (RAYN FOR-ests) Thick forests that receive a large amount of rain during the year.

real estate (REEL es-TAYT) The business of selling land and houses.

sea level (SEE LEH-vul) The height of the top of the ocean.

symbols (SIM-bulz) Objects or pictures that stand for something else.

timber (TIM-bur) Wood that is cut and used for building houses, ships, and other wooden objects.

tropical (TRAH-puh-kul) Having to do with the warm parts of Earth that are near the equator.

Index

A
Arctic Ocean, 4, 12, 16
Asia, 4, 20
Atlantic Ocean, 4, 12

C
California, 10, 16
Canada, 10, 12, 14, 18, 20
Caribbean Sea, 12
Central America, 12, 14, 16, 18

D
Death Valley, 10

G
Grand Canyon, 10
Greenland, 10, 12, 14

H
Hawaiian Islands, 4

I
Indian Ocean, 4

J
Jones, Lucy, 22

M
McKinley, Mount, 10
Mexico, 12, 18, 20

P
Pacific Ocean, 4

Panama, 12, 14
Pangaea, 4
Panthalassa, 4

R
rain forests, 14, 16
Rocky Mountains, 10

S
San Andreas Fault, 4
Southern Hemisphere, 8
Superior, Lake, 10

U
United States of America, 10, 12, 18, 20

W
West Indies, 12, 14

Web Sites

Due to the changing nature of Internet links, PowerKids Press has developed an online list of Web sites related to the subject of this book. This site is updated regularly. Please use this link to access the list:

www.powerkidslinks.com/asc/namerica/